THE

FIRST HINDOO CONVERT

THE
FIRST HINDOO CONVERT

A MEMOIR

OF

KRISHNA PAL

GYAN

Published by

GYAN

Gyan Publishing House
5, Ansari Road
Daryaganj, New Delhi-110002
Phone: 011-47034999, 9811692060
E-mail: books@gyanbooks.com

Distribution Network
gyanbooks.com
India, USA, Canada, UK, Australia, France

ISBN : 978-81-212-9226-9 (PB)
First Published, 1852

2nd Impression 2023

Printed at: Gyan Press, Delhi.

THE FIRST HINDOO CONVERT
Author: KRISHNA PAL

The First Hindoo Convert.

KRISHNA PAL.

THE

FIRST HINDOO CONVERT:

A MEMOIR

OF

KRISHNA PAL,

A PREACHER OF THE GOSPEL TO HIS COUNTRYMEN
MORE THAN TWENTY YEARS.

Philadelphia:
AMERICAN BAPTIST PUBLICATION SOCIETY,
118 ARCH STREET.
1852.

PREFATORY NOTE.

IT is a well known fact that modern Christian Missionary Societies had their origin among the Baptists of England, who formed their Society—now exulting in numerous churches and schools, in many thousands of converts, and in a larger number of translations of the Scriptures than any other missionary society,—on a very small and humble scale in 1792. Their first missionaries, —the Rev. William Carey and Dr. John Thomas,—sailed for India the following year, and there labored, with others who followed them, amidst trials and difficulties almost unprecedented, for more than seven years, before a single individual was sufficiently decided to renounce caste and put on Christ by baptism. A sketch of the Life of the first Convert now invites the attention of the reader.

While this narrative strikingly illustrates the grace of God in at length giving success to the labors of his faithful servants, its subject gave a good promise of future conversions, and showed the character which the earliest converts of the mission might be expected to bear. Nor will the reader of the interesting volume detailing the life of the first Karen Convert, Ko Thah-Byu, in connexion with the American Baptist Mission, in Burmah, fail to be impressed with the striking similarity of these two men to each other. Such unity in divine operations clearly shows that the work is performed by the same Agent.

Moreover, the facts here narrated show the importance of "sowing beside all waters," and especially the desirableness of open-air preaching. For be it remembered, that the first salutary impressions on the mind of Krishna were made by conversation in the street. Let Christians learn from the whole the importance of zealous, prayerful, persevering efforts for the good of souls; and oh, let the unconverted reader, while he sees Krishna listening to the gospel the very first time it is presented to his attention, reflect on his own folly and criminality in having neglected it till now, and take care that a converted idolater does not hereafter condemn him.

B.

PHILADELPHIA, Sep. 3, 1852.

CONTENTS.

THE FIRST HINDOO CONVERT.

CHAPTER I.

Visit of Dr. Thomas to Krishna—his seriousness—conversion—baptism—happiness.

ON the twenty-fifth day of November, in the year 1800, Dr. John Thomas, a physician and Baptist missionary at Serampore, then a Danish settlement, in India, was called in to set a man's arm which had been dislocated. This man was called Kristno, Krishnoo, or more properly Krishna Pal. He was now about thirty-six years of age, and belonged to the caste of carpenters, for in India, from time immemorial, different classes of persons are separated from each other. One caste or class never associates with persons of another caste, and, from one generation to another, each family pursues the same business, and belongs to the caste to which all their ancestors were attached. Christianity is now rapidly abolishing this order of things; but probably generations will yet elapse before this system will be entirely destroyed, and men associate as on a level with each other.

After Dr. Thomas had administered surgical relief to this poor man, who had broken his arm by slipping from the tank in which he was going to bathe, he spoke to him of the more awful disease of sin with which he was afflicted, and of the infinite kindness of God in preparing a remedy for the soul; he explained to him farther, that God sends afflictions as a proof of his mercy, and intends that thus sinners should be brought to pray for pardon and eternal life. Krishna was much affected, and greatly wept. On the same day he was again visited by Dr. Thomas and Mr. Marshman, another of the missionaries, as Krishna says "with some pieces of paper in their hands. They asked how I was? I answered that my arm was fixed, but still was painful. They gave the papers to me and to the by-standers to read. In this paper I read that he who confesseth and forsaketh his sins, and trusteth in the righteousness of Christ, obtains salvation."

The next morning he was visited by Dr. Carey, and afterwards by the whole missionary family. His arm soon regained its former strength, and from this period his visits to the mission-house were very frequent. He, together with his wife, and her sister, soon began to feel a deep interest in the Gospel; so that when Dr. Thomas one day asked him if he understood what they said to him, his reply was, that the Lord Jesus Christ gave his life up for the salvation of sinners, and that he believed it.

A new state of things now began to dawn on that mighty continent. Krishna and his female relatives soon gave evidence that they had been brought by the influence of the Holy Spirit to the cross of Christ, and expressed their readiness in all things to obey his laws. They seemed to have learned that sin is a dreadful thing, and to feel joy in hearing of the salvation of Jesus Christ. The missionaries say, "we sat down upon a piece of mat in the front of Krishna's house, for they had no chairs. It was very pleasant.

To have natives who feel a little as we do ourselves, is so new and different, that the country seems to wear a new aspect." In prospect of these persons making a profession of religion, the missionaries wisely say, "We think it right to make many allowances for ignorance and for a state of mind produced by a corrupt superstition. We therefore cannot think of demanding from them, previous to baptism, more than *a profession of dependence on Christ, from a knowledge of their need of him, and submission to him in all things.*"

But even before baptism, more than one trial had to be met. Christianity knows no caste, and can never sanction its friends living apart from each other. Caste had always been a barrier to Hindoo improvement, and it had long been an opinion even of the wisest men, that it could not be broken down; but what cannot the omnipotence of Divine mercy effect? The work was easily done. Krishna and Gokul sat down to eat with the missionaries in public, by which act caste was abandoned. The servants, and all who witnessed it were astonished, as all had said, and even the missionaries had almost feared, that no one would lose caste for the gospel. These last now saw the day for which they had been praying and hoping for years, and concerning which they had met many disappointments. This insurmountable difficulty, as it had been considered, seemed now to give way without any effort on the part of the missionaries. "After all," as Mr. Ward observed, "God has done it with perfect ease. Thus the door of faith is opened to the gentiles: who shall shut it? The chain of the caste is broken: who shall mend it?"

Another trouble arose out of this. As soon as Krishna's conduct in renouncing caste was known, the whole neighborhood was excited; two thousand people assembled to pour out their anathemas on the new converts, and Krishna and his family were placed in confinement. They were, however, dismissed by the magistrate, with commendations of their conduct. They were again brought back to the magistrate, on a charge against Krishna, that he refused to deliver up his daughter to a man contracted in marriage to her. The Governor interfered, and set them at liberty, assured the girl that she should not be compelled to marry the man against her own consent, and declared his determination to protect them during the administration of baptism.

So far all now seemed happy; but as the time of trial arrived, the wife and daughter of Krishna, his wife's sister, and one or two others shrank, so that at the head of the water appeared only Felix, a son of Dr. Carey, and Krishna. This was about noon of Lord's day, December 28, 1800; seven years after the arrival of the missionaries in India. The morning service had closed in the house, the sermon by Mr. Ward having discussed the subject of Baptism, from John v. 39, "Search the Scriptures." We give the description of the scene in the river, immediately before the gate, as shown in our engraving.

"We then went to the river's side. The Governor, a number of Europeans, Portuguese, Hindoos and Musselmans attended.—We began by singing in Bengalee:

> "Jesus, and shall it ever be,
> A mortal man ashamed of thee," &c.

Brother Carey then spoke for a short time in Bengalee; declaring that we did not think the river sacred—it was water only; and the persons about to be baptized, by this act professed to put off all the debtahs (idols) and all sins, and to put on Christ. After prayer, he went down into the water, taking his son Felix in his right hand, and baptized him, using English words. After this, Krishna went down and was baptised; the words in Bengalee. All was silence and attention. The Governor could not restrain his tears; and almost every one seemed to be struck with the solemnity of this, to them, new and sacred ordinance. I never saw, even in the most orderly congregation in England, any thing more decent and impressive. Ye gods of stone and clay! Did ye not tremble when, in the name of the Father, Son and Holy Spirit, one of your votaries shook you as the dust from his feet? When Krishna came from dressing, and here it is a very short work, a German lady, who had been witness to the ceremony, took him by the hand, and held him for some moments; and though unable to make him understand a single word, I could see that she thanked him from her heart for renouncing the worship of devils. To see brother Carey leading down into the water, on the same day, his eldest son, a missionary at fifteen years of 'age, and the first converted native who had fortitude sufficient to renounce his caste, was indeed an interesting spectacle. Brother B. lay in the palanquin (carriage) to see it. In the afternoon the Lord's supper was celebrated in Bengalee, for the first time. 'How amiable are thy tabernacles, O Lord of hosts!' Blessed day!"

The "brother B." referred to in this quotation was the Rev. Daniel Brunsdon, a lovely young minister who had joined the missionaries from England, and who was now contending with consumption, under whose power he soon after yielded to the grave. A sentence or two from his description of the scene will not displease the reader. "The last Lord's day in 1800, a Hindoo, named Krishna, was baptized, together with Felix Carey, in the river opposite our own gate. This is the first Hindoo who has trampled on his caste for Christ's sake, and joined the standard of the cross. I did not hear him make profession of the name of Christ before the church, on account of my illness; but I was so far recovered as to be carried to the water side, to see this pleasing sight. It was a very pleasant sight indeed. In the afternoon the Lord's supper was celebrated in my room, that I might be present. Most that was said was in Bengalee, in which I think brother Carey was greatly assisted, indeed. The thanksgiving before receiving the cup was in both languages."

It will be easily supposed that the happiness of Krishna, was now great, and that he would go on his way rejoicing, especially when he found that his wife and her sister became from this time entirely decided for Christ. At the close of the hallowed day which witnessed his union with the Church, he declared that he "was full of joy;" when asked soon after, in the street, by a European, what he got by his profession of Christianity? admirably did he reply, that, "He got nothing but joy and comfort;" adding, "it was the work of love." Speaking shortly after at a conference meeting, he said, "When I am at work, my mind goes away from God, and I am sorry, and charge it not to do so. I say, O mind! why dost thou thus depart from Christ? Thou canst not be happy any where without him: I charge thee to keep close to him." In a word, he seemed to have fully imbibed the spirit described by Joymooni, his sister-in-law, when she said, "O yes, my mind's book is open, in which I write down every thing that I hear about Jesus Christ."

It will be pleasing to close this chapter with a hymn written by Krishna a few weeks after his baptism, and which was thus translated by the Rev. Dr. Marshman:

THE feeble vessel of my soul,
On life's deceitful shallows struck;
The foaming billows o'er it roll,
The sails are split, the masts are broke:
Yet why, my soul, this anxious fear?
Say, why thus sinking in despair?

If thou indeed wouldst cut the sand,
And heaven-ward urge thy future course,
Then hear! There's help divine at hand,
The shipwrecked sinner's last resource.
Then why, my soul, this anxious fear?
Say, why thus sinking in despair?

In faith, on Jesus loudly call;
This instrument thy bark shall move;
Thus let thy vessel floating fall,
And swim in boundless seas of love.
Then why, my soul, this anxious fear?
Say, why thus sinking in despair?

CHAPTER II.

Happiness in his domestic relations—His mind exercised on preaching—Letter to the Society—Commencement of his labors—His own account of his preaching.

It will be readily supposed that the circumstances we have already related, had greatly added to the personal happiness of Krishna. He is described by the missionaries as being a man of a most lovely disposition, and of very pleasing manners. The type of his piety was of the right kind, just what might be expected in a man whose heart had been first melted by the delightful message, "This is a faithful saying and worthy of all acceptation, that Christ Jesus came into the world to save sinners." His wife, too, a few years younger than himself, of small stature, but always cheerful and active, had embraced the gospel, and had been baptized, and transfused her heart into religion; *Joymooni*, the sister of

Krishna's wife, a woman resembling *Rasoo*, her sister, in cheerfulness and activity, had given her heart also to the Saviour, and zealously conversed with her friends and neighbours in opposition to idolatry, and in commendation of Jesus; his children willingly yielded to receive Christian instruction, and manifested much shrewd discrimination; and the voice of prayer and praise twice a day ascended from the altar of this family so recently redeemed from idolatry. Who does not feel that such a household, now right, and right for the first time, must be happy? If angels do indeed take an interest in human happiness, they must have rejoiced in such a scene, and have increased the joy of heaven itself by the description they bore of it to the foot of the eternal throne.

The following letter written by Krishna to the Society in England by whom the missionaries had been sent out and sustained, is a fine illustration of the power of religion over his heart, and cannot be read by the followers of Jesus without pleasure. The peculiar idiom of the Bengalee language is retained in the English.

SERAMPORE, Oct. 12, 1802.

To the brethren of the church of our Saviour Jesus Christ, our souls beloved, my affectionately embracing representation.

The love of God, the gospel of Jesus Christ, was made known by holy brother Thomas. In that day our minds were filled with joy. Then judging, we understood that we were dwelling in darkness. Through the door of manifestation we came to know that sin confessing, sin forsaking, Christ's righteousness embracing, salvation would be obtained. By light springing up in the heart, we knew, that sinners becoming repentant, through the sufferings of Christ, obtain salvation. In this rejoicing, and in Christ's love believing, I ob tained mercy. Now it is in my mind continually to dwell in the love of Christ: this is the desire of my soul. Do you, holy people, pour down love upon us, that as the Chatookee, we may be satisfied.* I was the vilest

* The Chatookee is a bird, which, it is said, drinks not at the fountain, or at the streams below ; but when it rains, it catches in its bill the drops as they fall from the clouds.

of sinners: He hath saved me. Now this word I will tell to the world. Going forth, I will proclaim the love of Christ, with rejoicing. To sinners I will say this word: hear, sinner, brother; without Christ there is no help. Christ, the world to save, gave his own soul. Such love was never heard: for enemies, Christ gave his own soul! Such compassion, where shall we get? For the sake of saving sinners, he forsook the happiness of heaven. I will constantly stay near him. Being awakened by this news, I will constantly dwell in the town of joy. In the Holy Spirit I will live: yet in Christ's sorrow I will be sorrowful. I will dwell along with happiness, continually meditating on this,—Christ will save the world. In Christ, not taking refuge, there is no other way of life. I was indeed a sinner, praise not knowing.

This is the representation of Christ's servant,

KRISTNO.

The spirit of religion is communicative. No man can be brought under its influence without an earnest desire for the happiness of others. We are not at all surprised, therefore, to hear that one evening soon after his baptism, Krishna said that "his chief thoughts now were about the salvation of others," nor that he addressed to Christ the language, "Come, and I will give thee a throne in my breast; there I will worship thee; and I will invite others to admire thine excellencies." Dr. Marshman writes in his diary, July 6, little more than six months after Krishna had united with the church:—"Conversing with Krishna, he said to me, 'As I lay musing one night, I thought thus: One or two of the missionaries are dead; Mr. Carey is much engaged at Calcutta, Mr. Marshman in the school, and Mr. Ward in the printing office. Bengal is a large country; how shall the people know about Christ? I would go to the end of the world to make his love known.'"

His activity in conversation with the natives now became incessant. The method of his intercourse with them is thus represented: A man said, "Well, Krishna, you have left off all the customs of your ancestors,—what is the reason?" He replied, "Only have patience, and I will tell you. I am a great sinner. I tried the Hindoo worship, but got no good. After a while I heard of Christ,—that he was incarnate, labored much, and at last laid down his life for sinners. I thought, what love is this! And here I made my resting place." Going on to speak of the contrast between Christ and the idols which he and his countrymen had been accustomed to worship, he says, "Now say, if any thing like this love was ever shown by any of your gods? Did Doorga or Kalee, or Krishna, [the god after whom he had been named—Krishna-pal,—one of the flock of Krishna,] die for sinners? You know that they only sought their own ease, and had no love to any one."

We have an account more fully in detail of the character of his conversations with his countrymen, which will be read with interest; and not the less so because we give it as much as possible in his own style. He was told that an old man and two other persons wished to hear something about the gospel. They had stopped at an adjoining house, and Krishna went to them. Sitting at the door, he asked them whether they were not come to see the idol Juggernaut, whose worship was then celebrating, and under the wheels of whose car hundreds crushed themselves to death. They replied in the affirmative. Let us listen to the conversation:

Krishna.—What fruit have you found in this worship?

Byraggee.—None. What fruit have you found then, Krishna? Speak.

Krishna.—Byraggee, hear! The good news hear! Jesus Christ, the great Saviour, was not known in this country hitherto; but now the news of him is come. He, for the sake of his *enemies*, gave his own soul. His fruit is this: when a sinner believes in him, he gets the pardon of his sins, and a new mind. Christ is a place of refuge; there is no other place of refuge in the whole world, but him.

Byraggee.—This is astonishing love!—True, Krishna, this kind of love I never heard of before.

Krishna.—Byraggee, hear! We are all the children of God. In what manner? The same as a rich man who had two sons: his youngest went to his father for his share of the inheritance, telling him that he intended to go and live in another place. His share receiving, he went to another country: there staying, all his riches he spent; so that he became very poor. In that country a great famine happened: he had no money, no food, nothing at all. At length he became servant to a rich man, to feed his swine. He was full of sorrow: no means to preserve his life: what could he do? He ate with the swine. Now he remembered, and said, 'What do I? I have a father, a very rich father; here I all this affliction get.' His father being in his mind, he resolves to go. 'I will say, ha! father! I am a very wicked son: I went from you. Now, father, pardon my sins, my wickedness: give me something, or I perish. I will become your servant; you have many servants: only give me something to save me from perishing!' Thus thinking and resolving, he set off to his father. His father, a great way off, saw him. Seeing him, he said, 'Come, my son, my lost son!' The father great love showed, fell on his neck, and kissed him. Hear, Byraggee, in this manner we are the lost sons of God. He is our Creator; our Father. We have cast away our God; we know him not; we are a great distance from him. Now he is calling us, and saying, 'Come, my lost sons, come: I will not cast you away: I love you greatly!'—In this manner, Byraggee, God is calling to us by Jesus Christ.

Byraggee.—You have done well, Krishna; shame, fear, hatred forsaking, you have obtained the riches of Christ. Now, having heard of this astonishing love of Christ, I will certainly come to you and believe in him.

Alas, that we are compelled to say that Krishna, like other preachers, often failed of success. The old man wanted to unite Christ and his debtahs, or idols, together, and finding he must forsake all for Christ, he became discouraged and went back.

About this time, Krishna, prompted with holy zeal, without the least hint being given to him by any one, built a house for God, immediately opposite his own residence. Dr. Marshman says, "We call this *the first native meeting house in Bengal*, and intend to give him something towards the expense. To-day brother Carey preached in it to about twenty natives, besides the family of Krishna." In this house they held almost daily worship.—Here is a specimen, given by Mr. Ward:—"Felix [Carey] read the Old Testament, in Bengalee, morning and evening, at Krishna's place of worship. It gave me pleasure to observe that our Hindoo brethren and sisters were much moved with the affecting history of Joseph and his brethren."

"Let all the heathen writers join
To form one perfect book;
Great God, if once compared with thine,
How mean their writings look!"

The reader will not be displeased if we here introduce a rather long extract from a letter written to a gentleman in England, by whom he was supported in his itinerating labors for many years before his death. It gives, in his own words, a sketch of his ministry for a series of years:—

After this, the pastors of the church sent me and Gokool [another native convert,] into Jessore to publish the Gospel. They told us to publish the glad tidings through the death of Jesus Christ without fear, and gave us a number of tracts to distribute. On our way thither, in several places, we published the word. I had a letter of introduction from Mr. Carey to the Judge, which I presented to him. When the Judge had read it, he said to me, "are you Baptists ?" We answered in the affirmative. He asked us what we wanted. I said we wished to distribute the tracts which we brought with us, and which were extracts from the Bible. He told us we might give them to those who asked for them. After this we went into the town of Sahebgunj, and I read the fifth chapter of Matthew, and expounded it. Many people heard me and took the tracts. In the evening several brahmins came to the house we had put up at, and said to us, "Sircars, we are come to ask you a question: will the lands of the brahmins remain or not ?" We answered, "We know nothing about that, but we have come to seek the salvation of the souls of men." They inquired what that was. We then gave them the history of the birth, life, death, resurrection and ascension into heaven of Jesus Christ. They inquired, if there was no salvation in their religion. I said, "O Sirs, examine, and hold that which is right. Among you sin is not forbidden, and no hatred of it enjoined. In your poorans,

Ramayun, and Muhabbharut, there are no directions for the forgiveness of sin, and no knowledge of holiness, but an account of the incarnations and power of your gods: can man be saved by them?" They said, that if a sinner at the time of death repeats the name of Ram or Krishna, his sins will be forgiven, and he will obtain heaven. We said, that if that was sufficient to obtain salvation, pilgrimages, gifts to brahmins, alms to the poor, and the daily worship were useless. Moreover, the blind could not lead the blind, for both would fall into the ditch. What, were not Ram and Krishna men? Ram destroyed the race of king Ravun, and Krishna killed his maternal uncle and a woman. Are these gods? They then said, "These people are the destroyers of caste," and went away. We returned to Serampore. About a year afterwards, Mr. Marshman, brethren Seetaram and Kooveer [other converted natives,] and I went again into Jessore. In the town of Sahebgunj, on the market day, Mr. Marshman stood on his palankeen* and preached; many heard, and the

*A covered carriage, used in India, borne on the shoulders of men, and in which a single person is conveyed

market was almost deserted: the overseer of the market went immediately and complained to the Judge, that a Sahib [Englishman,] and three Bengalees had created a disturbance in the market, so that there was nothing sold or bought. The Judge sent two peons,* and had us brought to him. Mr. M. and Seetaram went into the Judge's house, and I and Kooveer remained without. While Mr. M. was taking a luncheon with the Judge, Seetaram was asked by one of the native writers there, whether he was a Christian? When Seetaram had told him he was, the writer beat him, and tore off his necklace, and turned him out of the house. Seeing the distress of Seetaram, I went to his assistance, and was served in the same manner. Mr. M. seeing this, endeavored to bring us into the Judge's house, when he was treated in a similar manner. After worship in the evening we returned to Serampore.

I have been unable to mention all my journeys with Messrs. Carey, Marshman, and Ward:—On one occasion, I went with Mr. Chamberlain to a fair at Gunga-Saugur, and

* Pronounced *punes.* Hindoo constables.

we distributed tracts there. After this I went again with Mr. Chamberlain to Dinagepore, and after remaining there fourteen days with him, left, and went to Benares, and on the way spoke and preached at various places. I was there five days, and spoke and preached the Gospel. There the brahmins said, I was a man from Serampore, and had been destroying the caste of several people there, and was come to do the same at Benares. They took me to the watch-house. I had with me three hundred books in the Nagree character. I was asked by the police native officer why I came to Benares, and I told him the object of my mission. He took a Bible from me, and read it, and appeared much surprised at it, and told me to go to the Judge at Secrole, and get his order for distributing these books. A peon was sent in charge of me, and ten or a dozen of the above brahmins went with me to Secrole. I put the passport which Mr. Carey had given me, and a Bible into the Judge's hand. He read the passport, and asked whether I were a Christian, and advised me not to remain in that part of the country, as the people would injure me. From thence I went to

Ramnugur, and preached before a rajah's house about Christ's incarnation and atonement for the sins of mankind. I again returned to Serampore.

The Missionaries agreed to my living in Calcutta, which I did for five years. In rotation I used to preach in twenty houses, and occasionally in different parts of the city. During my residence there, many Europeans and natives were baptized.

After this, by the desire of the Missionaries, I went with a native brother to Sylhet. I had a letter of introduction to Mr. Smith of that place. In my journey I stopped and preached at Dacca. There some of the most respectable Mussulmans sent for me, to whom I gave a Persian Bible, and lodged with them ten days. Proceeding from thence, I made the word known at Ajmeer and Baitool. At Chatuk I met with Mr. Smith. After reading the letter, he returned it to me, and also gave me another to the Judge of Sylhet. When I arrived there I gave the Judge the letters, and, on his inquiring, told him the reasons of my coming into that part of the country. Mr. Smith arrived at Sylhet a few days after. The Judge desired to see the books I brought with me, and was much pleased with them, and told me to give them to those who wanted them. I preached and distributed the tracts there.

The Judge wished me to go into the Khasee country, and gave me introductory letters to a jemadar and subadar there, and also a Sepoy,* as a guard. I was three days in going to that country. The jemadar and subadar gave me a lodging. I made known the glad tidings there. There I hope four sepoys and two natives of the Khasee country, and a native of Assam, were converted. After a few days, the Judge and Mr. Smith arrived there. I told them that I was very glad, for my labors had been successful. They requested to see the above-mentioned seven people, and inquired of them whether they believed in the death of Christ, that he died for sinners, and whether they wished to be baptized. The gentlemen then wished me to baptize the seven men, and had a silver basin, filled with water, brought on the table, and requested me to begin the

* A native infantry soldier in the British service.

ordinance. I told them I had never seen baptism performed in that manner. Upon their inquiring about the mode I followed, I referred to the baptism of John mentioned in the New Testament. They then said, I might do it in the way I preferred, and we went to the Dhuvuleshwuree river. There were present eight rajas, and about six hundred Khaseeyas. I read the sixth chapter of Romans, expounded and prayed, and then baptized the seven men. I remained in that part of the country eight months, proclaiming the Gospel, and then returned to Serampore.

After this I took a journey to Cutwa, Beerbhoom and Berhampore, and baptized a woman at one of those places. I was three months out at this time.

My next journey was to English-bazar, where I lived six years, and baptized a man and a woman. I then went to Dinagepore, and baptized four men and women there, and married two couples, Mr. Fernandez, the pastor of the church, being at that time ill. I again went to English-bazar, and was there till the next year, when I again journeyed to Dinagepore.

While I was there this last time, Mr. Fernandez baptized twelve persons, one of whom was a writer under the Judge. My grand-daughter being taken ill of a fever here, I was under the necessity of going to English-bazar to the doctor; fourteen days after my arrival there she died. On her death-bed she requested me to read the Bible to her and pray for her, and I trust she departed this life with a lively faith in Christ. I returned to Serampore after eight months. Then, at the request of the Missionaries, I went and lived two months at Dacca with Mr. Leonard, and there preached the Gospel.

I was baptized in 1800, and from that time to this have been employed in the service of God. Pray for me that I may live a little longer, and that I may still be employed in the same work with all my mind, and that I may always enjoy the communion of the Holy Spirit. I am now preparing to take another journey to Dacca. I was formerly dead in the worship of idols, but believing in our Lord, Jesus Christ, the Son of the living God, I am no longer dead. You have employed me in making the Gospel known to those who are dead in sin. O pray that God may preserve me, and crown my labors with success. I hope at the last to be received into eternal happiness."

CHAPTER III.

Krishna's first sermon—Interview with Gokol—Baptism of his daughter—Striking simile—Hindoo wedding—Supper party—Christian funeral—Dr. Carey's testimony—Ordination and settlement at Serampore.

We shall now go back to gather up and connect a series of facts relating to the life and ministry of Krishna, which he has himself omitted, but which were furnished by the European missionaries.

The first of these is a description given by Dr. Marshman, under the date of January 29, 1804:—"Intending to call out Krishna [into the work of the ministry] shortly, we desired him to preach to our servants. He accordingly delivered what Brother Carey calls the best Bengalee sermon he ever heard; fluent, perspicuous, and affectionate, in a very high degree. How different does the news of salvation sound in the mouth of a native, whose hope and joy it is, from what it does when delivered in our foreign and uncouth accents! And what a favor, as well as ground of encouragement it is, that He who ascended on high, and received gifts for men, should thus vouchsafe them to his infant church in Bengal!"

Mr. Ward, speaking of a difference of opinion between Krishna and one of his brethren, which for a time produced some alienation, describes Krishna as going to his brother and saying, "Gokol, lay aside your anger against me, and pray for me, as I have prayed for you continually. Remember the sufferings and death of Christ: remember them continually: your mind will then become tender: long-suffering, and compassion, and truth will abide in your mind." Gokol had formerly suffered great losses in business. Krishna told him of Job. 'First one messenger came,' said he, 'then another, and then another, to tell him of the loss of his all; yet after all he said, Naked came I out of my mother's womb, and naked shall I return thither: the Lord gave, and the Lord hath taken away; blessed be the name of the Lord.' Krishna still hopes of Gokol that his mind is towards Christ. He says also, that several neighbors are concerned about salvation; saying, 'we have been great sinners,—what shall we do?'"

The Christian parent who reads these pages, as well as the young Christian, will cherish feelings of holy sympathy in the perusal of an extract from a communication made by Dr. Marshman to Dr. Ryland: "Krishna's daughter, Golook, gave in her experience. The substance of it was, that she had heard the gospel from her father when we first came hither, and felt convinced that she needed such a Saviour as was therein revealed, and found her mind cleaving to him. When carried off by her husband, she still continued in her attachment to Christ, was once heard praying to him, and was beaten by her husband for so doing; after which she used to pray silently. When they repeatedly urged her to eat things offered to their idols, she as constantly refused; saying, that these could do nothing towards salvation, Christ alone could save. She appeared much impressed with the idea of joining the church, and was heard in prayer a good part of the preceding night." She was baptized, no doubt to the grateful delight of her father, a few days afterwards by Dr. Carey.

"This morning," writes Mr. Ward, in 1803, "Krishna came and told us of a conversation which he had with two of the Hindoos, named Kassinaut and Sheetaram, in which he used this simile:—the Hindoos, when they have built a new house, consider it unclean and untenantable till they have performed an offering; and then they take up their abode in it. So God does not dwell in earthly temples, however magnificent; his residence is in the heart. But how shall he dwell with man?—The sacrifice of Christ must be offered: then the house, the heart, in which this sacrifice is received, becomes the habitation of God through the Spirit."

To our younger readers it may not be unpleasant to look in on Krishna and his family, especially as we may thus be spectators of a wedding. The account is from the pen of Mr. Ward:—This morning early we went to attend the wedding of Kristno Presaud with Onunda, Krishna's second daughter. Krishna gave him a piece of ground adjoining his dwelling, to build him a house, and we lent Presaud fifty rupees* [about twenty-five dollars] for that purpose, which he is to return monthly out of his wages. We therefore had a meeting for prayer in this new house, and many neighbors were present. Five hymns were sung; brethren Carey and Marshman prayed in Bengalee. After this we went under an open shed, close to the house, where chairs and mats were provided; here friends and neighbors sat all around. Brother Carey sat at a table; and after a short introduction, in which he explained the nature of marriage, and noticed the impropriety of the Hindoo customs in this respect, he read 2d Cor. vi. 14–18, and also the account of the marriage of Cana. Then he read the printed marriage agreement, at the close of which Kristno Presaud and Onunda, with joined hands, one after the other, promised love, faithfulness and obedience, they then signed the agreement, and brethren Carey, Marshman, Ward, Chamberlain, Ram Rooteen and others, signed as witnesses. The whole was closed with prayer by brother Ward. Every thing was conducted with the greatest decorum, and it was almost impossible not to

*Silver coin of British India.

have been pleased. We returned home to breakfast, and sent the new married couple some sugar-candy, plaintain, and raisins; the first and last of these articles had been made a present of to us, and the plaintains were the produce of the mission garden.

We may be gratified with an account of a supper party on the following evening, given by the same pen:—This evening we all went to supper at Kristno's, and sat under the shade where the marriage ceremony had been performed. Tables, knives and forks, glasses, etc., having been taken from our house, we had a number of Bengalee plain dishes, consisting of curry,* fried fish, vegetables, etc., and I fancy most of us ate heartily. This is the first instance of our eating, at the house of our native brethren. At this table we all sat with the greatest cheerfulness, and some of the neighbors looked on with a kind of amazement. It was a new and very singular sight in this

*A stew of fowl, fish or meat with plenty of gravy, and eaten with boiled rice. More strictly, the gravy itself is the curry. Hence they say, "curried fowl," &c. This gravy or curry is made in various ways, but generally of sweet oil, red pepper, ginger, garlic and turmeric.

land where clean and unclean is so much regarded. We should have gone in the daytime, but were prevented by the heat and want of leisure. We began this wedding supper with singing, and concluded with prayer. Between ten and eleven o'clock, we returned home with joy. This was a glorious triumph over caste. A Brahmin married to a Soodao, [a low caste] in the Christian way; Englishmen eating with the married couple and their friends, at the same table, and in a native house. Allowing the Hindoo chronology to be true, there has not been such a sight in Bengal these millions of years! "Kristno," says Dr. Marshman, "seemed quite alive and happy, and I have seldom felt more so at a friend's table in England."

It was about this time that Krishna was induced by the Missionaries entirely to relinquish his secular engagements, and give himself wholly to Christian labor. For the support of himself and family, including his travelling expenses, they gave him, when from home about six dollars a month, and when he spent any time with his family, only half that amount. Such, or little more was the salary he received from this period till the close of his life.

As we have introduced our readers to a wedding, it may yield us both instruction and profit to attend a Christian funeral in that distant land. We borrow a part of the graphic account furnished by Dr. Marshman. After describing the death of a native Christian, and the tranquil and happy state of his mind, which made even his heathen neighbours say, one to another, "may my mind be as Gokol's was," he goes on to say,—Knowing the horror the Hindoos have for a dead body, and how unwilling they are to contribute any way to its interment, I had the coffin made at our house, the preceding day, by carpenters whom we employ. They would not, however, carry it to the house. The difficulty now was, to carry him to the grave. The usual mode of Europeans is to hire a set of Portuguese men, who live by it. But besides that our friends could never constantly sustain that expense, I wished exceedingly to convince them of the propriety of doing that last kind office for a brother themselves. But as Kristno had been ill again the night before, and two of our brethren were absent with brother Ward, we could only muster three persons. I evidently saw the only way to supply the deficiency; and brother Carey being from home, I sounded Felix and William, and we determined to make the trial; and at five in the afternoon, repaired to the house. Thither were assembled all our Hindoo brethren and sisters, with a crowd of natives that filled the yard, and lined the street. We brought the remains of our dear brother out, whose coffin Kristno had covered within and without with white muslin, at his own expense; then, in the midst of the silent and astonished multitude, we improved the solemn moment by singing a hymn of Kristno's, the chorus of which is "Salvation by the death of Christ." Bhyrub, the Brahmin, Peero, the Mussulman, Felix [Carey,] and I took up the coffin; and with the assistance of Kristno and William [Carey,] conveyed it to its long home; depositing it in the grave, we sang two appropriate hymns. After this, as the crowd was accumulating, I endeavored to show the grounds of our joyful hope, even in death, referring to the deceased for a proof of its efficacy: told them that indeed he had been a great sinner, as they all knew, and for that reason could find no way of salvation among them; but when he heard of Jesus Christ, he received him as a suitable and all-sufficient Saviour, put his trust in him, and died full of tranquil hope. After entreating them to consider their own state, we prayed, sung Moorad's hymn, and distributed tracts. The concourse of people was great, perhaps five hundred; they seemed much struck with the novelty of the scene, and with the love which Christians manifest to each other, even in death; so different from their throwing their friends half dead and half living, into the river; or burning their bodies, with, perhaps, a solitary attendant.

Dr. Carey seems to have written to his brethren in England less frequently than the other missionaries; but when he did write, his words were weighty. "Kristno," he says, towards the close of 1803, "has been ill some time past, but is now recovered. On the whole, we derive increasing pleasure from him; he appears to make solid advances in the knowledge of the gospel; and making it known to his perishing fellow countrymen seems his beloved employment." And again, he says a few weeks afterwards, "I went a journey in July last, for about twelve days, preaching in many villages, and giving away tracts. Kristno accompanied me, and rejoiced my heart."

In repassing over our ground in which we have trodden nearly in the footsteps of the different missionaries, we are again brought to the ordination and first settlement of Krishna in the ministry. Under date of February, 1804, Mr. Chamberlain wrote to a minister in London, "Yesterday, had you been at Serampore, your heart would have rejoiced. It was our ordinance [communion] day. The afternoon was set apart for praying in a special manner, for a blessing on *our* endeavor to promote the work of God, and for the calling out of two of our Hindoo brethren to the work of the ministry, Petumber Singho, and *Kristnoo;* both of whom we hope, are first called of God for this important purpose. They were set apart by prayer and the laying on of the hands of the brethren. After which, brother Carey addressed them from the text, 'As the Father sent me, so send I you;' and the occasion was concluded by the Lord's supper." And in the following May, Mr. Ward writes,—

"We had a long consultation about Kristno, and that part of the mission with which he is connected. It is absolutely necessary to have a native family at Serampore, to break the distance between the natives and us; to entertain inquirers from a distance, and to afford continual means of instruction to new comers. They do not understand our words so well, nor can they open their minds so freely to us as to our native brethren. In these respects Kristno and his family greatly serve the mission. We have not that leisure which is requisite for young inquirers, who are in a state of utter darkness respecting the doctrines and precepts of scripture. Almost all our members lately have been brought forward in their first impressions through Kristno and his family: sometimes they sit up a great part of the night with a new comer."

In Serampore, where he was now placed, Krishna labored with success for four years. We cannot but sympathize with a newly arrived missionary, who wrote the following year to his late pastor in England,—"I am persuaded that I have seen and heard such things since I arrived here, as would rejoice your heart, and the hearts of all those who love our blessed Lord, and long for the coming of his kingdom. What more pleasing sight could we behold, than that of a man, who a short time since was an idolatrous Hindoo now preaching the gospel to his deluded neighbors!—The native brethren supped with us on the night of our arrival. Krishno returned thanks to the Father of all our mercies, and sung two or three hymns."

CHAPTER IV.

Baptism of Krishna's son-in-law—Is persecuted—Krishna's illness—Testimony to the native preachers—Krishna's removal to Calcutta—His incessant labors—Mr. Ward's testimony—His views of missionary duty—Krishna's labors and usefulness—Dr. Marshman's testimony—Krishna's letter to a gentleman in England—Dr. Carey's letter to Mr. Sutcliff—Other letters from Krishna to England—Labors of native converts—Visit to Ugrudweepa—Conversions and baptisms—Krishna's letter to Mr. Skinner.

WE have in some degree anticipated, in our second chapter, an account of the ministry of Krishna, not only in Serampore, but in Calcutta also, where he afterwards successfully labored for five years. A large portion of the letter from which we there quoted, related to his labors before his ordination, and we were unwilling to destroy the beautiful narrative he gives us, in his own simple manner, of his ministry. Asking the reader to refresh his memory by again perusing it, we shall now endeavor to supply a few omissions.

The persecuting character of Mohun, the husband of Krishna's eldest daughter, has been already shown, and the fact of his giving great grief to all the parties concerned will not be disputed. But a proof was to be given, in his person, of the power of Divine grace to convert even an enemy like him, and bring him to a state of reconciliation with God. Messrs. Ward and Marshman say, under the date April 7, 1805: "Mohun, Golook's husband, has been some months with Krishno, and has appeared to lend a favorable ear to the gospel. Indeed he has publicly declared among Mr. Rolt's workmen, whose servant he has been for many years, that he will renounce Hindooism and embrace the gospel. His father-in-law, and our other brethren, whom we consult on every occasion of this nature, have a favorable opinion of him. We had a meeting before breakfast this morning for humbling ourselves before God, on account of the deadness of the cause among us. After this, Mohun, having previously made profession of his faith in Christ, was baptized in the river. He acknowledged his sin in his former violent opposition to the gospel, but said he did it in ignorance. His account of a change of mind was, upon the whole, pleasing and satisfactory; and if it be what it at present appears, it is among the wonders of grace. Instead of his compelling Golook to be an idolator, he himself is constrained to become a Christian! After Bengalee worship, a native came to one of us, and with tears talked of what he had been hearing. This day has been a kind of refreshing after the many disappointments we have lately experienced."

The mother, and other relatives of this young man, afterwards tried, in every possible way, to remove him from the influence of his Christian associates, and to induce him to renounce his faith in Christ; happily, however, they did not succeed. His mother took him before the chief magistrate, but as he declared his resolution to be a Christian, the magistrate declined all interference, except to assure Mohun that none should injure him.

During the period when these things were going on, the missionaries were one evening much alarmed by two of the native Christians, who ran into the house crying, "Krishna is dying! Krishna is dying!" Four of the brethren immediately went to his house, and found him somewhat relieved from a sudden and violent attack of illness. Dr. Marshman, evidently under some alarm, writes, "If the Lord should take him away, it will be a trying providence to the church, and an occasion of joy to Satan, if he knew what joy was." Four days after this, which was the Lord's day, Mr. Ward visited Krishno, and found him much better.

A few months after this, we have an account from a highly intelligent Christian gentleman of the character and preaching of Krishno and two other native ministers. He told us, says Dr. Marshman, a variety of interesting particulars respecting our native brethren, who for the last six months have been laboring in Malda. His intimate acquaintance with the Bengalee language enables him to judge with accuracy of their preaching; and he says that their knowledge of the gospel, shown in their discourses, united with their perspicuous and earnest delivery, would not disgrace a pulpit in England; that they are heard with great attention among their countrymen; that a congregation of *five or six hundred* often assemble to hear them, and this when no European is present to affect them by his influence; that some of the rich natives listen to them with apparent pleasure; and that some of them in a village near Malda kept one of the brethren nearly three weeks among them. He adds that many around his neighborhood are as fully convinced of the folly of idol worship as he himself is. His opinion coincides with that which I have long entertained, *that the effectual spread of the gospel in India will be chiefly by the instrumentality of native converts*, and that no means can be more adapted to the end. There is something in the presence of an European which excites a degree of fear and suspicion; but with their own countrymen they can be familiar.

We have already intimated that at the end of four years, Krishno removed from Serampore to labor at Calcutta, where he continued five years. A view of him here, given by Mr. Rowe, one of the missionaries, a part of whose family now resides in this country, will be read with interest:—Our dear brother Krishno has removed from Serampore to Calcutta, where there is a large field for missionary exertions, for which he seems well adapted. He is in his element when he is talking to a multitude of souls about their everlasting concerns. He is much esteemed by persons of different nations, as well as by many of his own countrymen, and numbers hear the words of eternal life from his lips. He has been to the jail at Calcutta several times. The jailor and his wife have joined the church. He is a very serious man, and feels much interested in the eternal salvation of the servants and of the prisoners committed to his care.—The tender mercies of God towards this our friend have been, and we hope will long continue to be the means of conveying the glorious light of the glorious gospel of Jesus Christ within the massy doors of this prison.

Last Lord's day I went to this prison to converse with four European young men, who are confined for murder, and whose trials will commence in a few days. Others of my brethren also attend them. To see the jailor weeping over the prisoners committed to his charge was enough to move the tenderest feelings of the heart.

Krishna has often been to converse with

both the servants and the prisoners. Twice he had them all together, and preached to them. His congregations here were formed of English, French, Armenians, Portuguese, Mussulmans, and of other nations. He had a long conversation with a Hindoo and a Mussulman. He faithfully warned them that if they continued to sin, they would go to hell, where the mercy of God would never reach them: but he showed them how the mercy of God was united with justice in the death of Christ, and entreated them to be reconciled to God.

While he was expounding the thirteenth chapter of the epistle to the Romans, a man said to him, "Brother, you speak good words, and have much wisdom; but why have you thrown away your caste?" Krishna answered, "The man who keeps his caste cannot obtain salvation. Men who have their caste are very proud, and he who is proud cannot enter into the kingdom of God. And like as an earthly judge condemns a Brahmin for a crime the same as a Soodra, so in the day of judgment will God judge men according to their works, and not according to their caste. All will receive according to their deeds. God will then forgive none."

After this Krishna dined with a Frenchman, and a number of other Europeans. To these persons he said, "You call yourselves Christians, but you do not keep the commandments of God. If you quarrel, fight, lie, swear, commit adultery, and other sins, you cannot be Christians. These are the works of the followers of Satan, and not those of the followers of Christ. Christians have love, unity, truth and holiness." After pointing out the evil of the vices to which he considered them as most addicted, he directed their attention to "the Lamb of God, who taketh away the sins of the world."

One or two of our Calcutta friends who have been lately baptized, are employed in the Dispensary. Krishna often goes to visit them, and by this means has an opportunity of talking to a number of natives there, as he has also to those who are employed at the custom-house. After reading to them out of the fifth of Matthew, he said, "You see the words of Jesus Christ are not like those of the Shasters.* I have done all your works and my sins did not go away; but from the time that I first heard of Christ's taking away sin, I have had great happiness of mind. My own works, wisdom and holiness are nothing; it is Christ alone that can save me. When I see sin, I am much afraid of it. I once acted according to my wicked desires, but now I have the fear of God in my heart, and am therefore afraid of sin. I am all sin of myself. Pride, anger, and every evil is in my heart; but God enables me to overcome them."

At the close of this discourse, many desired him to come another day, saying, "We will bring some wise people to talk with you about these things." A few days after, Krishna went again, and had a considerable number of people of different classes to hear him, among whom were several rich natives. One of them enquired who he was. He answered, "I am Krishna the carpenter; but I have now given over working at my trade, and am engaged in preaching the gospel of Jesus Christ. Behold, I now eat with all kinds of people.—

*A term applied to a book containing the institutes of the Hindoo religion.

This is according to the commandment of God, who has enjoined us to love him, and to love our neighbors. All are my neighbors. I am over none. I call none little folks. I am ready to be your servant for Christ's sake. I entreat you to turn to Christ."

A Brahmin said, "You have thrown away your caste that you might eat all kinds of flesh." Krishno replied, "I did it not for this; I am indifferent about what I eat." When he had ended his conversation, some of them invited him to their houses, and he told them that with pleasure he would visit them.

Mr. Ward speaks of Krishno, generally at this time spelt *Kreeshno*, and connects with this reference to him some remarks just as applicable now as then, and which we therefore quote:—Kreeshno has his hands full at Calcutta every day. We have not those rapid and numerous conversions we might wish for; and those who set out as missionaries with such expectations, will commonly be disappointed. If we would acquit ourselves as good soldiers of Jesus Christ, we must sit down and besiege the city, resolving to take it. If it do not fall during our life, we must recommenc the work to survivors with our dying breath. Missionary societies too, I think, should lay their accounts to go on with the work from generation to generation, and make the sending out of missionaries as much a part of their regular and necessary work, as the church does the sending out of ministers at home; and the collecting for missions as much a piece of regular work, as the collecting for places of worship at home. In short, it is a work which belongs to us and to our children, and to our children's children; as much a matter of course, as that after your minister, some one should be chosen to succeed him; and after the death of his successor, some one else to succeed him. Such appears to me to be a right view of the subject. The alterations produced in Bengal by sixty years English government is very great: sixty years more, accelerated by the progress already made, may produce much greater. And why not expect the same in the progress of Christianity? Some may say the time for the conversion of the heathen is not come. The time for multitudes to be converted under one sermon may not be come; but the time is come to do the work which God hath given us to do. He hath given us our work, and will do the same for our successors. To each succession of men he will give their proper work, and at the proper time that kind of success which some persons now demand, as a proof that the work is at all begun, will be afforded. 'Every man in his own order.'"

It will not be understood that these judicious remarks were written by the zealous missionary either as an apology for missionary inefficiency, or as a reason why Krishna in particular did not meet with more success. An extract from Krishna's pen, addressed to a friend in England, under date of May 23, 1810, will show that his labors were abundant, and we shall soon see also that they were successful:—"I was an idolater. I lived continually in sin. I was floating in a sea of sin. God, in great grace, made known, in the province of Bengal, the good news of the death of the Lord Jesus Christ, and is now preparing his chosen ones to perform his service. At present, he hath fixed me in this city; and I am now making known, week by week, the good news in the houses of forty-one brethren. I was lately preaching in the house of Mr.———, when his Hindoo servants assembled and heard the word. I was declaring, that in the whole world there was not one righteous person; but that all, having broken the law of God, were unclean. One of the servants, an old man, on hearing these words, was full of wrath—"What," said he, "is there not one righteous person among us? Gunga-govinda, Gour-mullika, and Nimoo-mullika, who are giving immense sums to the poor, are they not righteous?" "Ah, sir," said I, "All these things are ineffectual." At this they were still more enraged. I then made known the way of salvation through the death of Christ, in which the justice and mercy of God harmonized; and added, "They who see their sin, will come to Christ for salvation."

Formerly it was not known in this country, how men might obtain salvation; but now, through the great favor of God, in almost every house in the city, men are speaking of these things. Many come to worship, many are hearing and examining, and many are baptized. I preach to the debtors in the jail, and tell them of the good news of salvation by the death of Christ. I have also sung, and prayed, and preached, in the house of correction, among the thieves. Many of them have heard the news about Jesus Christ with joy, and were anxious to be instructed. I was ignorant through sin; through Christ I have obtained the true knowledge." Who that reads this account will hesitate to believe Dr. Marshman's statement, during the same year, "Several of our brethren evidently increase in Christian experience, and a deep sense of Divine things. Among these our beloved *Krishnoo* shines preeminently. His whole soul seems to be in his work; and his amiable and upright conduct gains the esteem of many who love not the gospel."

Persuaded as we are that our readers must best love to read of the "labors more abundant" of Krishna in his own beautifully natural and simple style, we shall give a translation of one of his letters, written about October in the same year as the last, addressed to a gentleman in England:—

Worship was performed at the house of Mr. Thomas Kaitauss. Mrs. Wilson used to come, but did not give her mind to what she heard. One day I read and preached from the eighth chapter of John, about the woman taken in adultery. Mrs. Wilson had formerly lived in an improper way with an European. The words of our Lord to this woman, "Go and sin no more," impressed her heart. Through this word God turned her mind, and she has since been baptized in the name of the Lord Jesus.

I was carrying on worship at Mr. Gilbert's at nine o'clock, and making known Christ's death and sufferings, and sorrows, from Luke xxiii. 32–43. Mr. Charles Pigott came there about some worldly business, but on hearing this sermon, he said, "This is the truth. I am a great sinner. Except Christ there is no deliverer." In this manner God bestowed his grace upon him; and he also was baptized.

Two men, the name of the one is Rada Krishna, and of the other Suda-Shiva, had heard the good news of Christ's death in the district of Jessore. Afterwards they came to Calcutta about some worldly business, and here sought after the gospel of Christ's death. They came into the chapel one Lord's day, and said, "Let us hear something of your religion." I then preached from Romans xii. 1, 2, "I beseech you therefore, brethren, by the mercies of God, that ye present your bodies a living sacrifice, holy, acceptable unto God, which is your reasonable service. And be not conformed to this world: but be ye transformed by the renewing of your mind, that ye may prove what is that good, and acceptable, and perfect will of God." These persons believed this word, and began to visit me, and do now eat and drink with me.

On Lord's day, at eight o'clock, I preach at the chapel, and again at four in the afternoon. On Monday, at four in the afternoon, I preach in the jail, and at seven in the evening at Mr. Pogus Petruse's. On Tuesday, I preach at nine o'clock in the morning, at Mr. Gilbert's; in the afternoon at Mr. Humphrey's; and at six in the evening at the chapel. As often as they can, the brethren Marshman and Ward preach this sermon at the chapel on Tuesday evening. On Wednesday, at nine in the morning, I preach at Mr. Charles Pigott's; at four in the afternoon, in the chapel; and at six in the evening at Mr. Thompson's. On Thursday, in the morning, I preach at Mr. Leonard's charity school; and at seven in the evening, we have a prayer meeting at the chapel. On Friday afternoon at four o'clock, I preach at Mr. Jefferson's; and at seven in the evening, at Mr. Thomas Kaiton's. On Saturday, at six in the evening, I preach at Mr. Kramer's. At the same hour brother Sebuk-Ram preaches at Mr. Cumberland's, at Cossipore. In this manner at present, is the kingdom of God making progress. This information I have given. This is Kreeshnoo the Christian's petition.

Nearly a year after this, Dr. Carey writes to his dear friend, the Rev. John Sutcliff, in a manner which equally illustrates his own simplicity of piety, and the Christian zeal of the subject of our memoir: 'Krishnoo labors at Calcutta with great success. He is a steady, zealous, well-informed, and I may add, *eloquent* minister of the gospel. He preaches, on an average, twelve or fourteen times every week, in Calcutta or its environs. Calcutta is three miles long, and one broad, and very populous; the environs are crowded with people, settled in large villages. The first is about a mile south of the city; at nearly the same distance are the public jail, and the general hospital. Brother Gordon, one of our deacons, being the jailer, we preach there in English every Lord's day. We did preach in the Fort; but of late a military order has stopped us. Krishnoo and Sebuk-Ram, however, preach once or twice a week in the Fort notwithstanding; also at the jail; in the house of correction; at the village of Alipora, south of the jail; at a large factory north of the city, where several hundreds are employed; and at ten or twelve houses in different parts of the city itself. In several instances, Roman Catholics having heard the word, have invited them to their houses, and having collected their neighbors, have received the word with gladness.

The number of inquirers constantly coming forward, awakened by the instrumentality of these brethren, fills me with joy. I do not know that I am of much use myself, but I see a work which fills my soul with thankfulness. Not having time to visit the people, I appropriate every Thursday evening to receiving the visits of inquirers. Seldom fewer than

than twenty come; and the simple confessions of their sinful state, the unvarnished declaration of their former ignorance, the expressions of trust in Christ and gratitude to him, with the accounts of their spiritual conflicts, often attended with tears, which almost choke their utterance, present a scene of which you can scarcely entertain an adequate idea. At the same time, meetings for prayer and mutual edification, are held every night in the week, and some nights, for convenience, at several places at the same time; so that the sacred leaven spreads its influence through the mass.

As no part of this little volume can be more interesting to its readers than Krishna's own simple and touching narratives of his labors, we shall make no apology for introducing one or two more of them. Writing in October, 1811, to a friend in England, he says;—We have, for some time, been preaching the word at the house of Captain M., at Calcutta. His wife was formerly a Roman Catholic, and an enthusiastic adorer of the crucifix and images, but through the grace of God, she has been turned from her error; has broken to pieces her images and crucifix, and is now a serious hearer of the gospel. Captain M. seems to be a sincere Christian, and his son and daughter-in-law have been lately called to the knowledge of the truth.

We have been preaching the word at Mr. Leonard's also, for a long time. His house seems to be a general rendezvous for the friends of Jesus. Many have been baptized, and many more are anxious for baptism; who received their first impressions there. The Lord has certainly given us abundant fruit to our labors in Calcutta.

At the jail we have constantly divine worship, and not without some effect. Many there hear the word attentively, particularly one Radha-churun, who was confined for a debt of seventeen hundred rupees [about eight hundred dollars.] He has been delivered from imprisonment; but how, or by whom, he does not know. Mr. Gordon, one day asking him how his debt was paid, he replied, "The same hand that redeemed my soul from everlasting flames, has now released my body from the jail." Happening to be there one day while he was present, I said, "Since we both believe in the same Redeemer, what harm in eating together?" Upon this he drank a cup of tea with me, and seemed very friendly. He is a constant attendant upon divine worship, and the Lord seems to have shown him the evil of his ways.

At Brother Kaitan's, our labors have been abundantly repaid in the success which has attended them. First, Brother Johan's, then his mother, and then his brother Kaitan, was baptized; then Kaitan's wife, and lastly, his servant.

Providence has lately taken from me my grand-daughter Pran, who died at the age of five. For some time before her death she seemed to love the Saviour. During her affliction, which was long and painful, she was never heard to murmur, but would often cry out, "Lord have mercy on me! Lord forgive my sins." To one who asked her whether she wished to live, and serve God here on earth, she replied, "I wish to go to heaven, and praise Christ there." Two days previous to her death, she called Anunda, and begged her to sing and pray with her, in which she also joined, kneeling down on her bed. Just before her death also, she got some friends together to read the scriptures, and sing, and pray with her; and while in this act she breathed her last, without a sigh or a groan.

Writing again in the following month, he says:—Returning from Brother Kramer's, I met Abdulla Mushee, and Moulobhee Elatonee, who took me home with them, and related the sufferings which they had endured for Christ's sake. Elatonee, a respectable Mussulman, was an inhabitant of Lucknow, but was obliged to flee to Calcutta on his becoming a Christian. The Mussulmans at Calcutta, hearing of his connexions at Lucknow, and also of his having become a Christian, were exceedingly enraged, and carried him before the police judge, declaring that he was insane. But he reasoned with the judge respecting the Koran, and declared before the whole court that he was sure Mahommed would never save him from hell; that Christ became incarnate to save him, and by trusting on him he hoped to obtain salvation. The Mussulmans were now more enraged, and prevailed upon the judge to send him to prison. They also declared, that until they heard from his family at Lucknow, they would not suffer him to become a Christian, but would rather take away his life. Some well-disposed persons, hearing of the affair, wrote to the judge, expostulating with him, and urging that if any Hindoo became a Mussulman, no one was suffered to molest him; why then should this man receive any molestation, who had of his own free-will left his family, his caste, and his religion, and upon the conviction of his own mind, had embraced Christianity? He was soon after this released from jail.

Abdulla Mushee is a Mussulman, a native of Delhi, but while residing at Cawnpore, heard the gospel from the Rev. Mr. M., and voluntarily renounced his caste, and made an open profession of the Christian religion. Fearing the Mussulmans at Cawnpore, he came down to Calcutta, where he now resides, declaring to all that he does not believe in Mahommed, but trusts for the salvation of his soul merely to the merits of Jesus Christ.

Maosee-bux, also a Mussulman, was formerly a servant on board a ship, but through some disease lost his sight, and is now obliged to procure his subsistence by begging. We have a rule to distribute on Tuesday afternoon, something to the poor, when we have an opportunity of dropping a word or two among them relative to the gospel. This poor man was among the number who came to receive alms, and was so impressed with a sense of his sin, that he has thrown off his caste, and made a profession of his belief in Christ, which has drawn upon him the frowns of all his former associates.

I one day asked him how he came to receive his first impressions. He said that when he heard of the great love of Christ for sinners, in leaving his throne above, and coming down to die for them, and reflected on his own dissolute life, he was so moved by a sense of gratitude, as well as by fear, that he was determined in the strength of the Lord, to renounce his caste, his connections and his sins, and, as a poor sinner, to throw himself at the feet of Jesus.

We have already introduced to the acquaintance of our readers Anunda, a daughter of Krishna, and Joymoonee, his sister-in-law, both consistent disciples of the Saviour. The following account written by Anunda, will show us the manner in which the native Christians, both men and women, communicate the gospel to their neighbors, and how the minds of many who are not decided Christians, are being detached from the superstitions of the country, as well as give us a view of Krishna, as usual, *at work.*

One day Joymoonee talking with a Hindoo woman concerning the gospel, the woman said that her gooroo [teacher] talked about these things to her and her friends, but that she could not understand what he meant. Joymoonee asked if she could see her gooroo? The woman answered that he sometimes visited at the house of Rasoo, her friend at Chinsurah, some miles above Serampore, where she believed he might be met with. After this, Joymoonee and two other sisters went to Chinsurah, to inquire for Rasoo. They asked a woman whom they met with near the place where Rasoo lived. She said, that a friend of hers, a religious man, was named Rasoo, to whose house she would conduct them, and they might then ascertain whether he was the person of whom they were in search. They found him to be that person, and he immediately bade them welcome. Joymoonee declared the gospel to them all; and the whole family seemed to receive it, declaring that this was what they wanted. The sisters stayed there that night. After this they made two other visits to this family, in one of which Rasoo said that when his gooroo came, he would introduce Krishna to him.

A little while after the gooroo arrived. He was a Brahmin of the name of Mohun-Mookhoojar. Being informed of what had occurred, he and his friends proceeded to Serampore, to see Krishna, who, on meeting them, declared at large the tidings of salvation.—They spent a day at Krishna's house, and from thence went to Calcutta, where this gooroo had many disciples. After stopping at Krishna's house in the city, the gooroo took him to the houses of several of his disciples, who on hearing him declared with much emotion, "This is the truth." They also made Krishna eat sweetmeats with them. It was then agreed among them to go to Ugrudweepa, where a feast was about to be held, to consult their *head gooroo*, who lived there.

On their way to Ugrudweepa, they called at Serampore, and took Krishna with them. He was glad of such an opportunity of declaring in the company of these friends, the glad tidings of salvation to the thousands assembled at the festival. Joymoonee and Komul also accompanied them. Of this journey Krishna gave the following account :—

In five days we reached Ugrudweepa. Here we met with brother William Carey, from Cutwa, and four native brethren with him. We were now eight Christians, and all put up at one lodging house, and ate together in the presence of all, who wondered to see an Englishman eating with Hindoos. At a proper season we went among the people, preaching the glad tidings of Christ's death for sinners. Some began to examine; some were aston ished; others appeared to receive the word.—I suppose thirty thousand people were present at this festival, in honor of Goopee-nat 'ha, a form of Krishna.

In the evening I went to the house of the head gooroo. He received me with much affection, and made me sit on the same seat with himself, declaring that he had wished to see me, and to hear of the faith of Christ. I read to him and explained the fifth chapter of Matthew, with which he was much pleased. He said, he was sure that this was the true religion, and that he would join us. He had separated, he added, from the idolaters around him, and wished to follow the true religion; but they were not of his mind; they persecuted and beat him; but still he was resolved to become the disciple of Christ. 'The caste,' said he, 'is not of God; I will therefore follow the Lord with you; for with you are all castes, Englishmen, Mussulmans and Hindoos.' At night about thirty of his disciples, Brahmins, rajpoots, weavers, gardeners and others, all ate together. He desired me to sit among them, and partake of the repast, which I did; and we praised God while partaking of this love-feast.

After we had all eaten, the head gooroo forbade Mohun-Mookhooja to invest his son with the poita, and the wife of Rasoo to give her sons in marriage among the idolaters. To a man present, whose name was Bhola-nat 'ha, he said, 'We will no longer preserve the distinctions of caste, but seek to possess the true religion, in which there is no caste. Come, let us walk in the true way; let us delay no longer.' His disciples all desired instruction from him, and assured him of a ready obedience. To me he said, 'I will consult with my disciples, come to you, and complete the work; for I assuredly know that there is one God, one religion, one Saviour, and no more.'

One incident connected with the conversation between Krishno and this head gooroo, as related to Mr. Ward, showed the ingenuity of the native missionary, and his power to produce a strong effect. Krishna saw a disciple of this head gooroo catch the water in his hands, as the gooroo, after washing his mouth, threw it forth; and sipping part of it, he rubbed the remainder on his head and breast. This water, that is, the water with which the gooroo has washed his mouth, they call *Udharamita*, or *the living water proceeding from the mouth.* Moved at this sight, Krishna, inwardly lamenting the pride of the gooroo, and the debased state of the disciple, mildly reproved the practice; and held up, as a divine contrast to it, the conduct of his heavenly gooroo, who washed the feet of his disciples. All present appeared to be much affected by the comparison.

A letter dated from Calcutta, in June, 1812, to his old friend and supporter, Mr. Skinner, of Bristol, will show the spirit of Krishna; and as this period closes his residence at Calcutta, we shall end our chapter with it. He says:

At present God is revealing his mercy to Bengal in a most encouraging manner. The class of religious mendicants called Utithis and Mushuntas have long been in search of the true religion, but knew not where to find it; but now, on hearing the gospel of Jesus Christ, they begin to think, 'What can we do? How shall we abide in the commands of this Saviour?' They frequently come to see us, and inquire more and more respecting the gospel: a few of them have been baptized. Among these leaders of sects, is Ram-doolala, who is said to have one hundred thousand disciples. They have no reverence for the gods. The name of a second leader is Neela-dasa, who may have five hundred disciples. These eat with us; but they say, 'If Christ has died for sinners, then there is no more sin in the world: why then do you go about teaching men that they are sinners?' To this I answer, 'If the debtor apply not to his surety, how can he be set free; and if men do not believe in Christ, how should their sins be taken away?' Another leader is Shiva-ramadasa, who has about five thousand disciples. For a considerable time past we have been preaching to them, and a few have been baptized. A fourth leader is Rusu-raja, whose disciples amount to about one thousand persons. Our brethren Chamberlain, and William Carey, junior, have had conversations with this man, and some of his disciples have been baptized. A fifth leader is Huri-dassa, who has about five hundred disciples, several of whom have been baptized, and there are hopes of the leader himself.

In a late journey to Jessore by Brother Carapiet and myself, we advised the deacons to spread the word through the villages around their own dwellings, and send their journals to Brother Petruse, at Chougacha. They readily agreed to this. From Chougacha we went to Koola-gachee, and remained two days preaching, and then proceeded to Vusi-poora, to the house of Prem-dasa, another leader of a sect, who was once under instruction at Serampore, and then advised some of his disciples to be baptized, namely, Shiva-dasa, Duyal-dasa,

Goura-dasa, and Nurottuma. After their baptism, Prem-dasa himself sought to be baptized, but was refused, as the woman he lived with was not his wife. Lately, however, Brother Petruse has married these two persons, and they have both been baptized. The people of those parts have been struck with astonishment at the conversion of this man, saying, 'Our caste must now go; he whom we regarded as a wise man has embraced this new way; what shall we now do?'

CHAPTER V.

Krishna visits Eastern Bengal—Letter from Silhet—Testimony of an English gentleman—Settled at Goamalty Journey to a Hindoo festival—Letter to Mr. Skinner—Residence at English Bazar—Last extract from his journal—Trials—Sickness—Death—Character, by Mr. Ward—Blessings of Christianity—Hymn.

EARLY in the year 1812, Krishno had expressed a desire to carry the gospel to the eastern borders of Bengal, where its light had never yet shone. This desire was encouraged by the brethren, and about March, taking the native Brother Gorachund with him, he departed. He paid two or three visits to Vasavayira, and helped them much who were resolving to cast their idols to the moles and the bats. He then proceeded on his journey, taking with him some tracts in the Assam language, prepared by the missionaries for that express purpose.

On the 7th of April, he wrote from Silhet: I remained ten days at Dacca, preached to many, and distributed about thirty books, and on the 20th arrived at Silhet. I was treated with the greatest kindness, and to many I gave books and made known the word. On the 8th of the following month, he thus writes:—Writes Krishna Pal. You will understand my prayer. The favor of God is fallen on this country: seven persons have been baptized: their names Prubhoo-singha, Gouree-singha, Rutuna-singha, Kumula-singha; these four are Sipahees; another is a native of Assam, his name is Vanee-Rama; and two others are Khassees, the name of one Dewankhasee, and of the other Ooana-khasee. All these persons have received the mercy of God; and others are hearing and receiving the word. The gentlemen here are preparing for me a dwelling house, twenty cubits long, and ten cubits wide, and for those who come for instruction, a house sixteen cubits long and eight wide. I have heard that my house is burnt down at Calcutta. I was a little grieved; but the Lord gave, and the Lord hath taken away.

Pray send a proper brother here, who

shall be able to instruct all these persons. After this I will come and take my family to this place. Consider of this, and write. I have thus informed you.

An English gentleman, writing to Dr. Carey, only three days after the date of the letter we have just given, says:—"I have the pleasure to transmit you the enclosed from Krishna, from whom you will perceive that he has made a tolerably good beginning in his present undertaking. I was present at the ceremony of baptism; many persons, particularly Khasees, were assembled to witness so novel a spectacle; and as novelty only seemed to bring them together, I was surprised to observe the decorum with which they conducted themselves. There were no attempts at ridicule; on the contrary, the impressive manner with which Krishna performed the service, appeared to me to have a sensible effect on the multitude, inasmuch as it seemed to compose their minds to the solemnity of the occasion. The Sipahee, who accompanied Krishna to Pandooa, was a Hindoo of high caste, a rajpoot, yet he was the first converted, and chiefly through his persuasion, his brother and two other Sipahees, shortly after embraced the same faith." The brethren at Serampore greatly rejoiced in Krishna's success, especially as the scene of his present labors was but a week's journey from China.

Not very long after this, we find Krishna at Goamalty, near the ruins of the ancient city of Gour. Here also his labors were successful, so that he soon organized a church of six members. And from hence he wrote the following account of a journey he made to a Hindoo festival, on the banks of the Brumha-pootra:—

On February 7th, I left English Bazar on horseback, and after staying one night at Dinagepore, I proceeded to a ghaut near Dhapa, a village in the district of Rung-poora, where, as I was eating, a man came, and asked me whither I was going. I told him that I was going to the Brumha-pootra festival, to declare the glad tidings of Christ's death, and distribute books containing the same news. This man, after hearing the word, went into the village, collected the people together, and told them that a man from Calcutta had brought many shastras; in consequence, in the midst of a circle of twenty-five persons, till late at night, I explained the gospel mystery, and showed them how justice and mercy had embraced each other in the death of Christ.—They appeared to receive the word with joy. I left them a New Testament and some tracts. Next day, at a shop in Rung-poora, I read part of the New Testament, endeavoring to apply it to the crowd who were present; many took books, and some said, "God has remembered us, for he has sent his mercy to us." I blessed God for putting these words into their hearts. At Alee-poo-ra also, the villagers assembled, heard the word, and accepted tracts in Naguree, declaring they had never heard this news before. After this in the market-place of Ranee-gunj, a large town, before a great company, I declared that the grace of God was come nigh unto them. They inquired what I meant. I then sat down at a corn-merchant's shop, and read the eighth chapter of Romans, which I explained to almost all the aged people of the place. They took a great number of books, and I blessed God, prayed for them, and left them. My next journey brought me to the bathing place, which was but six miles farther; the people were returning. I took up my station under a Banyan tree in a plain, and preached to about five hundred people, and distributed books. Some who received them came from Hindostan, and from the country of the raja of Vivat. On my return to Ranee-gunj, I found nearly two thousand people, among whom many books were given; as they were also at Alee-poora, and other places. I found many people sitting by the side of the river, at one place waiting for me, as they had heard that a person from Calcutta was preaching a new uvutasa, or incarnation, and giving away books. At another place where I stayed all night, I had much discourse with the inhabitants, and before I reached Dinagepoor, all my books were expended. There I stayed three days and preached, and in three days more arrived at home.

The station at Goamalty was occupied by Krishna for several years, and frequent were his journeys to and fro in the blessed work of preaching the gospel. Once more we introduce a letter from him to his old friend, Mr. Skinner:

The writing of Shree-Krishna-Pala: you will know my supplicating letter. Through the love of God, the grace of our Lord Jesus Christ, and the gift of the Holy Spirit, we are all well: you will be informed of this. More particularly; at the festival held at Sadoolla-poora, I read the fifteenth chapter of the first of Corinthians, and explained it in order.—But the Brahmins disputed about the doctrine of the resurrection; and asked, "Are our shasters then false?" To this I answered, "Oh! Brahmins, hear this comparison: the corn which you sow is not quickened except it die; and that seed which is sown, the same springs up: how then can you imagine, that after eighty lacs of transmigrations, you will be again born in the human shape, and that during these births you will be jackals, dogs, and other animals. How can this be? Therefore your own observations devours your shasters. The doctrine of the resurrection is not found among you; but now it is for the first time made known; and the resurrection through our Lord Jesus Christ is now published through the four quarters of the world. If you believe in the death and resurrection of the Lord Jesus Christ, you will obtain salvation; but if you do not, in no other way, in no other refuge, can salvation be obtained. This which I have told you is the true method of redemption." Before many other people I proclaimed the doctrine of the death of Christ, and gave away many tracts and books.

Secondly. At the festival of the new moon in Jishta [part of May and June,] at Ramakela, about ten thousand people assembled. I proclaimed in the midst of them the news of the death and resurrection of the Lord Jesus, and gave away books; but being fatigued, I sat down under a very large tree where many people came and inquired what the books were, which I was giving away. I said, "Oh, brethren! permit me to quote a verse which is current among you:—

The vedahs, the sages, the sects, the law-books,
Are all full of contradictions—
The way of the Great One that must be followed.

Therefore, brethren, who is this Great One? Among you there are three sects—the Shaktas, the Shivyas, and the Vishnuvus; but in these three sects not a person is to be found, of boundless truth, compassion and mercy. Yet in our Lord Jesus Christ these three qualities are complete: he is the Great One: and therefore I confess him, and, despising caste, family and honor, him I follow. He who believes in him shall inherit everlasting life; but he who believes not must endure everlasting misery." After I had said these words, some persons objected; but the Mussulmans defended me. Others said, "his words are right; for without perfect truth, compassion, and mercy, no one can be a Saviour." I have written this for your information. This: date, 21st June, [1816.]

In December, 1817, we find Krishna residing at English Bazar, a place of which we have already spoken, near Malda. His labors were incessant, but his success not very great; two persons, however, that year gave evidence of faith in Christ, who were baptized, and coöperated with him in Christian labors.

It will appear from the statements we have made, that Krishna carried the gospel of salvation from the mouth of the Ganges to Ben ares, and beyond the extremities of the East India Company's territories to the east, and that in nearly all these places he had seals to his ministry.

We now transcribe our last extract from his journal, bearing the date of May 11, 1818: —Shree Krishna Pal humbly writes: Through the grace of God, the Father, and of our Lord Jesus Christ, the writer is in a state of health and peace. More particularly, in two days we arrived at Bulurapore, where we put up at the office of the tax-gatherer, and proclaimed the glad tidings of the death of our Lord Jesus Christ. Very many persons heard the word. Secondly, we then proceeded to Kachunpore, where we saw that the people had set up three images, Chamar-Kalee, Lukshme, and Peirasur. Here we read the divine word, and prayed in the name of Christ, when all the people of the village abandoned the gods, and cried out, "Let us break down these places of the gods, that the gods may never come into this place again." Agreeable to these words, they broke down with their feet these places of the gods. After this we arrived at Dinagepore. A few days afterwards we crossed the river Atrace, where, at the Varoone festival, crowds of people assembled;

and here Nidhircam and Pudmulochun assisted me in publishing the good news of our Lord Jesus Christ's death, and in distributing many tracts. While thus employed, I met with Goluk-Mookoyya, a Brahmin, who said, "O brother, I do not serve the gods! Brumha God! let him be blessed: I serve him." I replied, "O Brahmin, God hears not the prayers of sinners: but they who through the atoning death of our Lord Jesus Christ pray, their words he hears. For except the justice and the love of God can embrace each other, sinners cannot be saved; but in the death of Christ these two are united: on which account God has appointed Jesus Christ to the work of a Saviour. Therefore they who have laid hold of the death of Christ by faith are saved." He then said, "I have an elder brother, if you can visit him at Ranee-gunj, he will be glad to see you." We assured him that we would visit there on Lord's day. We accordingly went, and I read from the third of John the account of the new birth. He, hearing, remained in silence, but convinced, and at length promised that he would go to the Sahib [Christian missionary,] at Dinagepore, and hear from him these words.

We next proceeded to Shickmurud fair, and, on the first day, arrived at Sadamuhul, and stayed there three days, during which time I held meetings for prayer and worship, and visited the brethren and sisters from house to house, teaching them the doctrines of the gospel. We then went forward to the fair, where I proclaimed the glad tidings, and gave away tracts. On the 29th of April, we left Dinagepore, and came to Katavave, where I made known our message, reading the first of John. All the villagers were assembled, and they asked us what they should do with their gods. I told them to believe in the atoning death of Christ, and they would obtain salvation. They then requested that I would give them some instructions from the holy book, and leave them in writing. I then wrote some passages from the twelfth of the Romans, "I beseech you, therefore, brethren, by the mercies of God, that ye present your bodies a living sacrifice to God, which is your reasonable service." Whosoever believes in the atoning death of our Lord Jesus Christ, upon him the gods can have no power, but he shall obtain salvation.' I added, "They into whose hands these instructions shall fall, after reading them, must copy and send them to the three next villages, or stand charged with guilt in the world to come, of the ruin of all those souls."

Such was the character and such the labors of the beloved Krishna; but his course was not all comfort and joy. He had severe trials, particularly near the end of his career. Especially had he to endure great domestic sorrows; besides all this, he was approaching sixty years of age, which in India is considered a very advanced period of life. In the summer of 1822, he became anxious to retire to some quiet retreat, where he might speak of his Saviour, and die in peace. That summer and autumn brought great sickness and several deaths to the missionary band, and while Krishna was forming his plans of future life, on Wednesday, the 21st of August, he was attacked by the fatal Cholera; and though his relations neglected too long to apply for medicine, yet at first the disorder appeared to give way to medical applications. The next day the medical gentleman residing at Serampore was called in by the missionaries; but he gave it as his decided opinion that the patient could not recover. Still Krishna lingered through the day, edifying all around him by his entire resignation; by the sweet tranquillity which illuminated his aged and languid countenance, and by the many refreshing words which he delivered respecting his own safety and blessedness in Christ. It appeared to be the feeling of all who visited him, "It is good to be here. Verily God is in this place. Let my last end be like Krishna's."

We quote now from the account furnished of the death and character of Krishna, by his friend and brother, the Rev. William Ward. The account derives additional interest from the fact that it was the last paper written for the press by that devoted missionary; who, a very few months afterwards, followed Krishna to his eternal rest. Speaking of Krishna, Mr. Ward says:—

When asked about his attachment to Christ, he said, "Where can a sinner go, but unto Christ?" And when the same question in another form was put to him, he said, "Yes, but he loves me more than I love him." The same question was put a short time before he expired by one of the missionaries when he nodded assent, and laid his hand on his heart, but was unable to speak.

The total absence of the fear of death was most conspicuous: when exhorted to take medicine, he objected to it as unnecesary and fruitless. But being pressed, he yielded, still positively forbidding them to give him laudanum, (though generally considered as a necessary part of the prescriptions for this disorder) as it would produce insensibility, and put a period to those comforts which he then enjoyed. He begged that those who prayed for and with him would not pray for his recovery; and once or twice he asked if the grave had been prepared.

He appeared to have conquered all his worldly attachments, declaring that he did not wish to remain any longer in this thorny world; that his Saviour had sent his messenger for him, and he wished to go.

Although his mind was thus weaned from the world, and delivered from all anxiety respecting the future circumstances of his family, yet he was concerned for the salvation of his friends; and hence, when asked by an attendant if he was desirous of prayer, he seemed pleased with the proposal, and said, "Pray that I may be saved, and that all my family may be converted;" thus exhibiting the last anxieties of a Christian parent, and pouring out his last breath for the good of those whom God had given him in the flesh.

Nor was Krishna, in these his last moments, unmindful of the cause of Christ in Bengal. He declared to those around him, that all he had he had received from Christ; and that it was his desire that it should be given back to Christ, and devoted to the spread of his gospel. Poor man! he had nothing to leave except the Chapel he had built near his own dwelling; but the wish to make some return to the Redeemer proved that he was sensible that the Gospel, introduced to his attention by Dr. Thomas, so many years ago, had done great things for him.

As *a private Christian*, Krishna stood high among his brethren, as well as among Europeans, by all of whom he was recognized as an upright and truly sincere and amiable Christian.

As *a preacher*, Krishna was truly evangelical in his views. He preached Christ, none but Christ, and Christ, the suffering, the atoning Saviour. He would often tell his countrymen how Justice and Mercy embraced each other in the undertaking of the Redeemer. He would contrast with wonderful effect, Christ washing the feet of his disciples, with the Hindoo spiritual guide, having his foot on the disciple prostrate at his feet. He would dwell with delight on the divine properties of the Redeemer, proving from thence that he only was the true Gooroo, (spiritual guide) and would confirm these descriptions by reading to his heathen auditors the Redeemer's sermon on the mount. His method was mild and persuasive: and the sight was truly edifying to see this Hindoo convert in his simple native dress in the pulpit pleading with his countrymen and for Christ's sake beseeching them to be reconciled to God.

Such then was the religion of this Hindoo convert: summing it up, it amounts to this confession: "O Lord, I was once a poor stupid heathen. I worshipped dumb idols, and knew not but that these were the true God. To remove guilt from my conscience, I bathed in the Ganges, I worshipped my teacher [Gooroo] and licked the dust of his feet; I gave my property to the priests; I visited holy places; I repeated the name of my guardian deity. And lest these acts of religious service should not prove sufficiently meritorious, I hoped for a son to perform those rites after death which might deliver me from any difficulties into which my spirit might fall after leaving the body. Thus blind I lived, and thus deluded I should have died. But, blessed be thou, O Father of mercies, I heard the tidings of mercy through an atoning Mediator. These tidings led me to a knowledge of my spiritual state; and I found myself lying under a dreadful load of guilt. By faith, I fled to the Lord Jesus for refuge from the wrath to come; and the Saviour gave me peace and joy in believing. Now it is my joy to speak of him, to spread the knowledge of his death, and to communicate his unsearchable riches to my poor countrymen. I love my Saviour, though not as he loves me. I find his promise good,

'I will not leave you comfortless.' I have no fear in death. My only wishes are, that I and my family may be his; that all I have may be devoted to him; and that I may depart and be with Christ which is far better."

Do any doubt, whether Christianity be a good worth bestowing on the Hindoos? Let them look at this simple account which this converted heathen has given of himself; an account which flowed spontaneously from his own feelings, and in writing which he was wholly left to himself, and had no expectation of its publication. Look at heathen Krishna receiving his idolatrous teacher, washing his feet, and anointing his head with the dirty water, and look at the same man sitting with his Christian pastor, or delivering a sermon from the pulpit. Look at heathen Krishna, repeating an unmeaning incantation, or teaching it to others as a religious nostrum—and see him afterwards surrounded with a group of heathens, reading to them the Beatitudes.—See heathen Krishna worshiping a wooden image of his lewd name-sake, and then look at the same man worshiping the true God, and pouring out his heart in prayer in the midst of his Christian brethren. Look at heathen Krishna while he joins in the filthy songs and dances in honor of his idol, and then hear the same man lifting up his voice amongst a congregation of converted heathens, and singing in the Bengalee a hymn, written by himself, of which a free imitation is annexed. Look at heathen Krishna overwhelmed with debt, and daily eluding his creditors, and then look at the same man punctually discharging all his engagements, and exhibiting through life the strongest contrast to the heathen in this respect.

Look at the heathen by the sides of the Ganges, calling upon their dying relations to repeat the names of Narayun, of Gunga, of Ram, and of a whole rabble of gods, pouring the waters of this river down the throat of the dying, exposing them in the agonies of death to the chilling damps by night; and to the scorching beams of the sun by day; and listen to the cries of the dying, "Tell me not of works of merit; I have been committing nothing but sin. And now—where am I going? —What is there beyond this wretched existence? Am I going into some reptile or some animal body; or shall I at once plunge into some dreadful place of torment? I see the messenger of Yuma [the king of death] coming to seize me. Oh! save me—save me! O mother Gunga give me a place near to thee. Oh! Ram! Oh! Narayun! O my gooroo [his spiritual guide] how dark and heavy the cloud which envelopes me—is there no certainty, no ray of light from any of the shasters to guide and comfort me in my departure? Must I take the irrecoverable plunge, to be seen no more?"——And when they have seen and heard all this, let them look at the death of Krishna, the Christian, consoled by the addresses of his Christian brethren, by the hymns which they sing, by the words of the everlasting Gospel which they repeat; and let them listen to the pleasant words which proceed from his dying lips: "My Saviour has sent his messenger for me, and I wish to go to him,"—and then let them say, Whether the Gospel be a boon worth giving to the heathen.

We close our volume with a hymn written by Krishna, very frequently sung in India, and a considerable portion of which is used in our own churches. We doubt not but the history of its author will invest it with new interest in the esteem of the reader:—

O Thou, my soul, forget no more,
The Friend who all thy misery bore;
Let every idol be forgot,
But, O my soul, forget HIM not.

Bruhma for thee a body takes,
Thy guilt assumes, thy fetters breaks,
Discharging all thy dreadful debt;—
And canst thou e'er such love forget?

Renounce thy works and ways with grief,
And fly to this most sure relief;
Nor Him forget who left his throne,
And for thy life gave up his own.

Infinite truth and mercy shine
In Him, and he himself is thine;
And canst thou then, with sin beset,
Such charms, such matchless charms, forget?

Ah! no—till life itself depart,
His name shall cheer and warm my heart;
And, lisping this, from earth I'll rise,
And join the chorus of the skies.

Ah! no—when all things else expire,
And perish in the general fire,
This name all others shall survive,
And through eternity shall live.

THE END.